CW00520643

the Witches' Love Spell Book

by

CERRIDWEN GREENLEAF

Running Press

PHILADELPHIA

Running Press
Hachette Book Group
1290 Avenue of the Americas, New York, NY 10104
www.runningpress.com
@Running_Press

Printed in China

First Edition: August 2014

Published by Running Press, an imprint of Perseus Books, LLC, a subsidiary of Hachette Book Group, Inc.

The publisher is not responsible for websites (or their content) that are not owned by the publisher.

Library of Congress Control Number: 2014935576
ISBN: 978-0-7624-5459-4
LREX
15 14 13 12 11

Lucky in Love:
RITUALS FOR ROMANCE

A S A TAROT READER, astrol-
oger, and magic-maker, I
do readings for friends old and
new and 90% of the time, the
questions are all about love.
And, I understand! One of the

main reasons I started studying
metaphysics and the magical
arts was to try and understand
the human heart. Like you, I had
first crushes that didn't pan out,
had my heart broken unceremo-
niously (and broke a few hearts
myself, I might add), and also
have experienced true love, that
dizzyingly wonderful feeling that
makes this old world go 'round.
I have found that a grasp of a few

magical and astrological basics go
a long way toward a happy love
life. The wisdom I have gathered
is in these pages to help you, dear
reader, become spellbinding to
any romantic interest and to have
a long and happy love life.

Love resides in a mystical
realm where two bodies, minds,
and souls meet. It's a heightened
state with raw emotions: to love
another person is to give yourself

completely, unconditionally. It is a chance to use every sense and every power you have. The magic within this spell book can help you turn the vulnerability of love into a sublime spirituality. All it takes is clarity, intention, and authenticity. Conscious love isn't a random act, but the result of focus and self-awareness.

Let this little spell book be your treasure chest of ideas. I

have arranged this guide from cre-
ating the setting and environment
for romance, to how to choose
your soul mate, how you can
attract anyone you desire, surefire
first date success, and spells for
every stage of love. Romance has
its ups and downs, to be sure, but
this compendium of charms will
give you an advantage in the field
of love (and help you through
the bumps). These incantations

and enchantments are tried, true, and tested by yours truly, and by trying them, you'll soon have your family, friends, and co-workers commenting on "how lucky in love" you seem to be. But you and I know we can make our own luck with a little bit of magic.

And this love-magic doesn't have to just be in the realm of relationships. Like I said, love makes the world go 'round.

Don't forget to use these amorous charms for the benefit of
others and the betterment of the
world. I encourage you to love
one another and share with one
another. I believe we all have
unique gifts and special talents—
harvest them and pass them
along. Spread the love!

Love by the Stars, the Sun, and the Moon

THE BEST RELATIONSHIPS happen when one person's Moon sign is the same as the other's Moon. Opposites also attract, as many a lusty Leo and quirky Aquarian can attest, so you should also check out the person right across from you in the zodiac. Some of the most delightful and exciting love can happen when people are very different and complement each other.

Fire Love:
SO WARM IT HURTS

FIRE SIGNS ARE INTENSE, usually positive, and often impetuous. Fire signs get things moving. They are passionate and need a match of enthusiasm in the bedroom. Fire signs belong together. Sparks can also fly if your Moon or Venus is in a fire sign.

♥ Warrior Aries anger easily,
  but the "kiss and make-up"
  part can be fun.

♥ Tell a Leo they are wonderful and you will be amply
  rewarded with fireworks
  between the sheets.

♥ Adventurous Sagittarians
  like to make love outdoors.
  I recommend a hike followed
  by skinny-dipping and a sexy
  "workout."

Air Love:
SMART IS SEXY!

AIR SIGNS ARE THE GREAT communicators and philosopher/techies of the zodiac. They are always thinking. These fun and social creatures really get along with everyone, although Earth signs may try to keep them too grounded.

♥ **Geminis** are very verbal
during intimacy, so a little
erotic talk can drive them
crazy with desire!

♥ **Libras** are the most partnership-orientated of all signs, so a very romantic approach will bode extremely well here. Libras are ruled by Venus and have refined love-making to an art form.

♥ **Aquarians** are wildly experimental. Together, you'll go through all the *Kama Sutra* positions and beyond.

Earth Love:
THE TENDER TOUCH

EARTH SIGNS ARE AT ONCE
solid and practical and extremely
sensual. Grounded and security-
orientated, they are the most
involved with the physical body
of anyone in the zodiac.

♥ Taurus is ruled by Venus, so they are very amorous. Bring a fine wine and some food into the bedroom for an "afternoon delight." Soft fabric, good music, perfumed oil—all senses are explored with Taurus Bulls in the bedroom.

♥ Virgos are not fussy neatniks; they are highly skilled lovers. Virgos are service-orientated— a wonderful attribute.

♥ **Capricorns** work just as hard
in the bedroom as they do
in the boardroom. Support
them as they strive for success and you will be amply
rewarded by an attentive lover
who will sweep you off for
weekend trysts.

𝔚ater 𝔏ove:
EMOTIONS RUN DEEP

WATER SIGNS ARE THE MOST
emotional and sensitive of the
signs. These people feel things
intensely and their empathy and
sensitivity can make for deep
exquisite love. A passionate
group, to say the least.

♥ **Cancers** are very nurturing; this is a lover that will take care of you and meet your every need, sexual and otherwise. They are home-orientated, so the bedroom should be a palace with every comfort.

♥ **Scorpios** are reputedly the most passionate of any sign—they are walking sex and they know it! They love mystery. In bed and out, they want to dominate and own you. Whisper in their ear that you want that, too, at the exact right moment for Ultimate Pleasure.

♥ Pisceans **are dream lovers, so intuitive they can anticipate your every need and give you unceasing sensuous attention. These trysting fish would never get out of bed if they didn't have to!**

Light of Love:
ALTAR DEDICATION

LIGHT THE CANDLES and incense and dab the jasmine and essential oils near your heart. Speak aloud:

I light the flame,
I fan the flame,
Each candle I burn is a wish
My lust will never wane.
I desire and I will be desired.
Harm to none, so mote it be.

Attracting
that Attractive
Stranger

THIS SUREFIRE ATTRACTION
spell will bring that stranger
to you. It is a "come-hither conju-
ration" with simple yet supernat-
ural magnetic pull. Use wisely!

Begin this ritual on a Friday, Venus's Day. You will need:

◊ mandrake root
◊ pink roses and candles
◊ two goblets of wine

Place on your altar a man or woman-shaped mandrake root. Place the goblets of wine beside it. Burn the candles every night for a week starting on a Friday.

Sop from the goblets and recite:

Merry stranger, my heart,
Merry may we meet again.
Hail, fair fellow, we'll meet
With this wine I toast you,
As we merry meet again.

Make sure you look your best,
and you will soon lock eyes again.

Budding Love:
NEW BEGINNINGS

THIS SPELL CAN BE USED to meet someone new or to bring on a new phase in an existing relationship.

You will need:

◇ one pink and one blue candle

◇ lily or jasmine oil

◇ cinnamon tea and cinnamon sticks

Anoint both candles with the essential oil. Light both and recite:

Healing starts with new beginnings.
My heart is open, I'm ready now.
Goddess, will you show me how.

Drink a cup of cinnamon tea that you stirred counterclockwise with a cinnamon stick. Sprinkle cinnamon at your front door. When the cinnamon is crushed underfoot, its regenerative energy will help you start a fresh chapter in your love life.

Two Hearts Beat as One

TO TRANSFORM THE OBJECT of your desire into your partner in passion, try this powerful attraction spell.

You will need:

◇ plain muslin cloth
◇ dried sage
◇ one seven-day pink candle
◇ red thread and needle
  or stapler

Take the plain muslin and cut
it into two heart shapes. Sew (or
staple if you are in a hurry) the
two hearts together and leave a
hole so you can stuff it with dried

sage. Then sew it shut and either write or, if you are really crafty, embroider the name of the object of your affection onto the muslin heart. Put it on your altar.

Each night at midnight, the witching hour, light the pink candle for thirty minutes beside the heart of the sachet and say aloud three times:

To ____ I offer affection.
To ____ I offer attention.
To ____ I offer joy.
And in return, I shall have the same.
So mote it be.

Now, your crush will return your attention and be ready to return your affection.

Amorous Amulets
(For Surefire First Dates!)

FOR AN OPTIMAL OUTCOME
to any important meeting—
whether in romance or not—take
an amulet with you. It can be a tiny
sack hidden in a pocket or con-
tained in a locket. Fill your amulet
with any of the following herbs:

FOR COURAGE:
try borage or mullein.

TO AVOID BETRAYAL:
*the snapdragon will serve
you well.*

FOR ROBUST HEALTH:
rue will do the trick.

TO OVERCOME NERVOUSNESS:
*a mix of dried yarrow and
nettle is potent.*

**TO IDENTIFY
ANOTHER WITCH:**
*ivy, rue, broom straw,
agrimony, and fern
work the best.*

FOR TRAVEL:
*always wear comfrey
for safety.*

FOR YOUTHFUL ENERGY:
*the oak's acorn will
vitalize you.*

**FOR STRENGTH
AND PHYSICAL STAMINA:**
*tuck some mugwort
in your shoes.*

TO ASSURE VICTORY:
*woodruff assures
a winner.*

**TO GUARANTEE A
FRIENDLY EXCHANGE:**
*heliotrope will make for a
good conversation.*

⤳ the ⤶
Enchanted Bed

ANOINT YOUR BED with this special charm. In a red cup, mix a half-teaspoon of rose oil with a half-teaspoon of jasmine oil. Hold it with both hands and speak:

In this bed, I show my love.
In this bed, I share my body.
In this bed, I give my heart.
In this bed, we are as one.
Here, my happiness lies as I give
and live in total joy.
Blessed be to me and thee.

As you say, "Blessed be," flick drops of your bed blessing oil from your fingers all across the bed until the cup is empty. Now, lie down and roll around in the bed. After all, that is what it is for!

Goddess Body Blessing Balm

CELEBRATE THE BEAUTY of your body. Your body will receive much attention during your lovemaking, so loving attention from you beforehand will consecrate the temple of your body.

Take one cup of natural bees-
wax, chip it into a double broiler
and heat very slowly and gently.

Add a quarter-cup sesame oil
and stir with a wooden spoon
until the wax has melted and
blended with the oil. Let it cool
to skin temperature and add:

- ◇ eight drops sandalwood oil
- ◇ five drops lemon oil
- ◇ two drops rose oil

Anoint yourself with the oil by dabbing a bit on your fingertip and then placing it on your heart, circling outward until your entire body is fully blessed. This should be done slowly, gently, and lovingly as you speak aloud:

We all come from the Goddess.
I am she and she is me.
My breasts are holy and
wholly beautiful.
I love myself, I love my body,
I am consecrated.
Lover, come to me now.

Aphrodisiacal Altar

TO PREPARE for new relationships and to deepen the expression of feeling and intensity of your lovemaking, you have to create a center from which to renew your erotic spirit—your altar. Here you can concentrate your energy, clarify your intentions, and make wishes come true! If you already have an altar, incorporate some special elements to enhance your sex life. As always, the more you use your altar, the more powerful your spells will be.

Your altar can sit on a low table, a big box, or any flat surface you decorate and dedicate to magic. Begin by purifying the space with a sage smudge stick—a bundle of sage that you burn as you pass it around the space. Then cover your altar with a large, red, silky-smooth fabric. Place two red candles at the center of your altar and then place a "soul mate crystal" at the far right corner. Soul mate, or twinned, crystals are any crystals that formed fused together. They are available at metaphysical stores.

Anoint your candles with jasmine and neroli oil. Keep the incense you think is sexiest on your altar, too. For me, it is currently peach and amber musk, which I simply love smelling. Your love altar can serve as a sacred space in your home from which positive energy flows.

Elixir of Love

ELIXIRS ARE VERY SIMPLE potions made by placing a crystal or gemstone in a glass of water for at least seven hours. Remove the stone and drink the "crystallized water." The water will now carry the vibrational energy of the stone, the very essence of the crystal. This is one of the easiest ways to "take in" crystal healing, and it is immediate. The red stones always hold the "lust for life," so to push the envelope, put as many red stones into your elixir as you can get your hands on. Place into a glass of water:

◇ carnelian
◇ garnet
◇ rough ruby

- ◇ red coral
- ◇ red jade
- ◇ jasper
- ◇ red sardonyx
- ◇ cuprite
- ◇ aventurine
- ◇ red calcite

Mix and match and remember, if you only have access to a rough ruby and a tiny chunk of jasper, so be it—that is still a *lot* of love in a jar!

Place the ecstatic elixir in the love corner of your room or on your altar. Light amber incense and a red candle and speak aloud: *This jade is my joy, the garnet my grace.*

Leave the water on your altar for seven hours or overnight and drink it upon awakening. Your life energy will quicken and you should feel very upbeat and "good to go!"

Love Nest Spell

To anoint your home a sacred space and turn it into a loving nest, rub any one of the following essential oils, undiluted, on your doorjamb.

- ◇ cinnamon
- ◇ clover
- ◇ cypress
- ◇ dragon's blood
- ◇ frankincense

Walk through the door and close it securely. Take the remaining essential oil and anoint every other door and window. At the witching hour, midnight, light anointed white candles and place

them in every doorway and windowsill, and sing:

*My home is my temple, and here
I will live and love and be healed.
And so it is by magic sealed.*

𝕳appy 𝕳ome
for 𝕿wo:
HOUSEWARMING RITUAL

WHEN YOU AND YOUR partner
move into a new home, place a
wreath or bundle of dried hops
and eucalyptus on the front door.
Walk through the door, light your

favorite incense and a brown candle, and lie down in the center of the front room. Whisper:

House of my body,
I accept your shelter.
House of my spirit,
I receive your blessings.
Home to my heart,
I am open to joy.
And so it is. And so it shall be.

See with Your Third Eye Ritual

SANDALWOOD, from the Sanskrit word *chandana*, has been used for thousands of years in India. The woody, sweet smell clears your mind and reconnects you to the Earth. It is a good

idea to be relaxed before you get
together with a special someone.

Anoint a brown candle with
sandalwood oil. In scentless base
oil, such as canola, olive, or sesame, add:

◇ six drops sandalwood oil

◇ two drops lemon oil

◇ two drops amber oil

Warm this concoction in a clay oil lamp or carefully heat it on the stove. When it is warm to the touch, dip your left ring finger into the oil and anoint your "third eye," located in the center of your forehead, just above the eyes.

Sitting in the cross-legged lotus position, whisper three times:

Come to me clarity,
come to be peace,
Come to be wisdom,
come to be bliss.

Meditate for twenty minutes, then massage the warmed oil onto your feet. You will be utterly, blissfully grounded now.

Is He "The One" For Me?

MANY WITCHES CARRY a pendulum with them at all times to help make the right decisions, especially when it comes to the question "is he the one for me?" They have recently become available at most metaphysical stores, but a lovingly handmade pendulum is imbued with more personal energy. Take a strong string or length of leather and tie a ring, gemstone, or crystal to the end.

By the light of the New Moon, take a bundle of sage, light one end, and pass the smoke over your pendulum, "smudging" and purifying your space.

Wear the pendulum around your neck for seven days. Each

night, light black candles on your altar to absorb negative energy and, holding the pendulum still, chant:

Guide me to the path of truth,
Goddess hear my song.
The pendulum I charge
with my energy,
To judge right from wrong.
So mote it be.

On the seventh day, you can begin using your new tool. Any time you need advice in the realms of love, dangle the pendulum and observe its movement— swaying from front to back means yes, left to right means no.

Color Magic: Heart Hues

COLOR HAS A PROFOUND effect on our psychological and physical health. Consider carefully the colors that surround you because each of us has special colors that encourage sound body and mind. For example, if you have a weight issue and lack ambition or energy, you may need more orange in life. Wear orange clothes and eat foods associated with orange, such as red plumbs and wax beans. Here are some basic color connections:

Pink is about love and romance. You can bring more of this into your life with red cabbage, beets, strawberries, and rose wine.

Violet is associated with senti-
ment, melancholy, and religious
devotion, and can be enhanced
by eating chocolate, thyme, and
scallops.

Orange, associated with abundance and ebullience, can be
absorbed through oranges,
squash, red plums, yeast, and
wax beans.

Yellow is connected to the renown, wealth, power, and excellence, and is best ingested through pumpkin, cheese, rye, oats, lettuce, and beer.

Color Magic Continued

Green, the color of everlasting
life, friendship, and optimism,
is concentrated in beef, alfalfa,
endive, and grapes.

Blue relates to humility, faith, and innocence, and is the mainstay of mint, garlic, radishes, sage, turnips, and peppers.

Red, associated with lusty power, success, and control, is best absorbed through cabbage, bacon, cherries, lemons, tomatoes, and paprika.

Body Glow:
PURIFICATION RITUAL

SALTS FROM THE SEA have
been used to decontaminate the
body, by way of ritual rubs, since
ancient times in the Mediterra-
nean and Mesopotamia. From
Cleopatra to Bathsheba, these
natural salts have been used to

exfoliate the skin and enhance circulation, vital to overall body health. There are wonderful imported Dead Sea salts readily available at most bath and beauty stores, or you can make your own "cupboard cure" which follows.

To prepare for your purification ritual, light lemon or myrrh candles, step out of your clothes, and hold the salts in the palms of both hands, praying:

Isis, in your wisdom help me
reflect your image;
My body is a temple to
the Goddess.
Here, I worship today with head
and hands,
heart and soul.

Use the salts with a new
loofah sponge and scrub yourself
vigorously during the waning
moon at midnight.

"I Feel Pretty!"

MANY WITCHES PREFER whipping up their own healing beauty magic. Here's a simple recipe for a homemade salt rub. The beauty of this recipe is that you can change the essential oils to suit your mood.

Combine:

◇ three cups Epsom salts

◇ one tablespoon glycerin

◇ four drops ylang-ylang

◇ one drop jasmine

◇ one drop clary sage

Mix well and store in a colored glass jar. Use these salts with the Body Glow Purification Ritual to help exfoliate your skin.

Venus Skin Beauty Lotion

YOU WILL NOTICE THAT many witches appear ageless. There is a good reason for this: We take good care of our skin and heighten the health of our complexions with a Venusian prescription for eternal youth.

Combine the following oils:

◇ two ounces sweet almond

◇ two drops clary sage

◇ two drops chamomile

◇ two drops myrrh

◇ two drops rosemary

◇ two drops geranium

Before you anoint your skin
each night, utter this spell:

*Goddess of Love, Goddess of
Light—hear this prayer.
Your youth and beauty eternal
please share.
So mote it be.*

Rub the potion on your face
and rinse off for healthy skin and
a radiant glow.

Elemental Magic for Love:

AIR

WIND, A MANIFESTATION of the element Air, is a harbinger for change. The west wind is especially potent for healing, while the south wind is known to bring new beginnings. You can carry this powerful instrument with you wherever you go by "capturing the wind" in a white cloth bag. While standing facing the wind, say this spell:

Brother wind, around us you blow;
All that is old and sad in this life
with you go.
After the storm, I stand in the rain;
I thank you for all that I gain.
With harm to none,
this spell is begun.

Tie the bag with a blue ribbon. Whenever you see a situation that could use a change for the better, you can "pour" some of the winds of positive change.

𝔈lemental 𝔐agic
for 𝔏ove:
⤙ EARTH ⤙

IF YOU ARE SOMETHING of a
gardener, you can symbolically
"plant" transformation into your
life. Take a handful of beans from
your pantry or a seed package
and empower them by placing

them on your altar during the
light of the waning moon. Plant
them after you have prayed:

I plant these seeds of fortune
and change.
As they grow, good luck for all will
rise and flow.
From this soil comes all bounty,
as we know.

Romance Remedies:

FLOWER ESSENCES

TO PREPARE THE FOLLOWING remedies, mix two drops of flower essence into 30 milliliters of distilled water. Take four drops of the remedy daily until your health is restored. You can also apply the remedy to your pulse points (wrists, temples, behind the ears, backs of knees), add it to your bath, or spray it into the air.

Addiction: skullcap, agrimony

Anger: nettle, blue flag, chamomile

Anxiety: garlic, rosemary, aspen, periwinkle, lemon balm, white chestnut, gentian

Bereavement: honeysuckle

Depression: borage, sunflower, larch, chamomile, geranium, yerba santa, black cohosh, lavender, mustard

Exhaustion: aloe, yarrow, olive, sweet chestnut

Fear: poppy, mallow, ginger, peony, water lily, basil, datura

Heartbreak: heartsease, hawthorn, borage

Lethargy: aloe, thyme, peppermint

Stress: dill, echinacea, thyme, mistletoe, lemon balm

Spiritual blocks: oak, ginseng, lady's slipper

Flower Charm

TO LIGHT THE FIRE OF LOVE in your heart, place a green candle beside a white lily, freesia, or a spicy-smelling stalk of stock (a plant in the mustard family) in the twilight of the New Moon. Make sure the flower has a scent you really love; the floral essence is the key to stirring your memories and dreams. For me, that is a gardenia floating in a clear bowl of water. White flowers usually have the most intense aromas. Anoint the candle with tuberose or rose oil. Take a handful of nuts from your kitchen cupboard and place them in front of the candle. Make sure they are still in their shells—walnuts, pecans, or pistachios will do nicely.

Honey Love Tonic:
INSPIRED TEA

BOIL ONE PINT of spring water.
Place into your favorite crockery
teapot a half-ounce of any one of
the following herbs: rosemary,
mugwort, yarrow, or thyme.
Steep for ten minutes and strain
with a nonmetallic strainer.

Cheesecloth is great, or try an inexpensive bamboo strainer. Sweeten with a little honey; I recommend clover honey because you get the added benefits of clover's lucky powers. Sip this brew while relaxing.

Messages from Your Mind:
SYMBOL WRITING

IF YOU WISH TO MAKE direct
contact with your unconscious,
here is a way to see through the
veil between two worlds and
enter the recesses of your mind.

It can be very helpful if you
are confused by the actions of
another and need advice from
the divine.

At any herbal store or metaphysical shop, obtain dried mugwort,
dried patchouli, or wormwood.
The latter is a bit harder to come
by, but worth the try. It is the
active agent in absinthe.

Crumble any one of these
herbs between your hands until
it is gently ground into an almost

powdery consistency. Pour the herb into a baking pan. Make sure the crumbled herb dust is evenly spread over the surface of the pan. Light yellow candles (from your creativity altar) and close your eyes. Take the forefinger of your left hand and touch the center of the pan. Run your finger back and forth in a completely random pattern—don't think, just rely on your instincts for two minutes. Open your eyes, look at the pattern you have drawn, and write down what the symbols and designs bring to mind. Also write down the thoughts you were having while you were "drawing." Some of my friends have found that they unconsciously wrote words, which they then used to start a poem or novel or which generated an idea for a painting.

Seeds of Change:
GROWING YOUR LOVE

NATURE IS THE ULTIMATE
Creator, and by making things
grow you will tap directly into
this life force. Get an array of seed
packets and start a magic garden
that will help you to sow fertile
new projects and get them off the

ground, so to speak. Try parsley, fennel, or nasturtiums (the easiest thing to grow, bar none).

On a New Moon day, draw a square in your yard or planter with a willow stick, oak stick, or wand and mark each corner with a candle—

◇ **one pink** *(for love)*

◇ **one red** *(for romance)*

◇ **one orange** *(for higher intelligence)*

- ◇ **one green** *(for creativity and growth)*
- ◇ **one blue** *(for serenity and goodness)*
- ◇ **and one white** *(for purification)*

Repeat this chant as you light each candle:

> *Mother Gaia, I turn to you*
> *to help me to renew,*
> *Under this New Moon and*
> *in this old Earth,*
> *Blessed be.*

Poke the seeds under the soil with your fingers and tamp them down with your wand. Gently water your New Moon garden and start a new project the very next day.

Charms for Love

ANOTHER CHARM for luck in love is to take seven tiny rose quartz stones and put them on your windowsill during a full moon for seven hours. Then pick up the stones and, while holding them in the palm of your hand, speak this wish-spell aloud:

Luck be quick, luck be kind,
And, by lucky seven,
good luck will be mine.
Blessed be.

Nature Lovers:
LUCKY TALISMANS

TALISMANS ARE CHARMS you can carry with you to help ward off ill fortune and attract the positive toward you. And what is more attractive to a lover than positivity? Here is an old-fashioned spell you can easily make from your pantry and garden.

On the night of the New Moon, stuff dried rose, acacia, and clover into a gold velvet or silk bag. Lastly, place a small magnet in the sack and sew it shut with a gold thread. Hold the bag over the smoke of white sage and incense, and meditate to purify your creation. Visualize blessings

for you and your loved ones.
Carry your lucky talisman with
you at all times and begin count-
ing your blessings.

Prophetic Dreams

TAKE A DRIED POPPY seedpod
and empty the seeds onto
the ground. Take a tiny strip of
paper and write down a question
about how to attain meaningful
and positive rewards in your life.
Sleep with the pod and the paper
under your pillow. You will

experience prophetic dreams
that will answer your question.
This is best done during the
Pisces Moon.

Keep a dream journal by your
bed and write down the dream
immediately upon waking. Make
this a ritual and you will have a
rich resource of inner wisdom to
guide you.

The Giving Tree

I N CELTIC LORE they were called wishing trees, and Taoists referred to them as money trees—either way, they can be giving trees. Plant one in your yard, or pot one for your home or office. If you have to rely on indoor gardening, the biggest

ficus you can find will do nicely
in a jade-green ceramic pot.
Choose from among these magical trees or trust your intuition in
arboreal matters:

- ◇ **Cherry** *(for romance)*
- ◇ **Peach** *(for love magic)*
- ◇ **Willow** *(for healing and broken hearts)*
- ◇ **Apple** *(for divination and spellwork)*
- ◇ **Oak** *(for strength and lust)*
- ◇ **Olive** *(for peace)*
- ◇ **Aspen** *(for sensitivity)*
- ◇ **Eucalyptus** *(for purification)*

Claim Your Splendor Spell

THROUGHOUT YOUR spell-working, make sure to maintain a sense of personal abundance and acknowledge the great spirit within you. Be grateful for your body and for your

health. Stand in front of the mir-
ror, preferably naked, and drop
all self-criticism. Concentrate
on your real beauty and envelop
yourself with unconditional self-
love. Wrap your arms around
yourself as you say:

In Her/His image, I, too,
am a Goddess/God.
I walk in beauty; I
am surrounded by love.
Blessed be.

Light three candles in your
favorite color and scent. Sit in
front of your altar and meditate
on what would make you achieve
your full potential.

Do you need to change your
health habits? Do you need to

open your creativity? Do you
need to revitalize with a vaca-
tion? Concentrate deeply, and
choose three wishes to write
down and place under your three
candles. Every night for seven
days, repeat this spell:

Today I arise.
This night I embrace
My serenity, radiance, splendor,
and wisdom.
Blessed be.

Wind-Borne Blessings:
LOVE ON THE WAY

PART OF EXPERIENCING life (and love) is recognizing the opportunities that literally lie in your path. When you see a bird's

feather on the ground, pick it up
and put it in your pocket and you
will have good fortune all day. An
eye to the sky will lend much wisdom if you follow this old lore:

- ♥ Birds flying on your right are a good sign.

- ♥ Birds flying on your left are inauspicious.

- ♥ Bluebirds, as the old saying goes, stand for happiness.

- ♥ Cardinals, or any red birds, stand for wishes coming true.

- ♥ Eagles are indicators of success.

- ♥ Ducks signify newfound love.

Leaf Love

HERE'S A SWEET BIT of alchemy available to all, handed down from medieval times. Wise women of old taught their children to watch for falling leaves. To catch one in midair is the best kind of luck, direct from

Mother Earth herself. Carry it
with you for a season and you
will be kept safe from harm
and will receive unseen rewards.
If you are especially blessed and
catch more than one falling leaf,
share it with the one closest to
you. You will be bound by both
love and fortune.

Lust Dust

NOWADAYS, YOU CAN BUY body glitter almost anywhere. I've noticed that we witchy types were way ahead on the glitter curve. Whether it is baby powder, a body glitter, or the edible honey dust sold by the inimitable Kama

Sutra Company, get a powder that feels comfortable on your body and add the following to it:

◇ **One drop of amber oil**

◇ **One drop of vanilla oil**

◇ **One teaspoon lotus root powder**

◇ **A quarter-teaspoon of cinnamon**

Stir or shake and let it dry out before stirring again.

Stand naked and gently rub the powder all over your body. All day or night, your skin will feel tingly and ever so slightly warm. Notice the interested glances wherever you go. Soon, your body will be a map for exploration.

Song of the Siren Spell

MERMAIDS AND SIRENS are extremely erotic symbols and each one of us can conjure their power. Buy a pound of sea salt at a grocery store and place it in a bowl with ten drops each of jasmine and neroli or ylang-ylang essential oil. Mix them together. Instead of a shower in the morning take a bath with your Siren Salts. While submerged, visualize that you are turning heads with your mesmerizing mermaid beauty and silence. When ready, rise up and do not comb or towel dry yourself or your hair—drip dry naturally. As you go through the day, do more listening than talking. The compliments and attention will amaze you!

Sacred Love Altar

AT YOUR ALTAR—your magical power source—you can "sanctify your love." Collect your tools, meaningful symbols, and sensual iconography and prepare for the sacred rituals of love.

Gather:

◇ red and pink candles

◇ incense

◇ Victorian violet and rose
  essential oils

Light the candles and incense
and dab the essential oils on
your chest, near your heart.

Speak aloud:

I light the flame of desire,
I fan the flame of passion,
Each candle I burn is a wish
And I come to you as a witch.
My lust will never wane.
I desire and I will be desired.
Harm to none, so mote it be.

Pillow Talk Charm

To SECURE LASTING, blissful love from a nascent romance, a love pillow can cast a powerful, binding spell. This spell works best if you use a soft, homemade pillow.

Gather:

◇ two yards pink satin fabric

◇ goose down

◇ dried red rose petals (best if you've grown or received from your lover)

◇ golden thread

◇ amber and rose oil

Take the satin fabric and stuff it with the goose down and the dried rose petals. Sew it with the golden thread while you whisper:

Here rests the head of
my true mate fair.
Nightly rapture is ours to share.
So mote it be.

Anoint the thread with amber
and rose oil, especially while you
"entertain." You can refresh the
threads from time to time.

Belles Lettres for Binding Love

LOVE LETTERS ARE an ancient art that always deepen intimacy. Create your own powerful love letter to grow your connection with your lover. You will need:

- ◇ special paper and ink
- ◇ perfume
- ◇ wax

Take a sheet of your special paper and write with a magickal colored ink, which you can either make yourself with berry juice or buy at the nearest metaphysical store. Perfume the letter with your signature scent or one your lover appreciates, like amber, vanilla, or ylang-ylang. Seal it

with wax you have also scented
with a drop of essential oil, and
of course, a kiss. Before your love
letter is delivered, light a candle
anointed with your preferred
scent and say:

> *Eros, speed my message*
> *on your wings of desire.*
> *Make my lover burn with desire.*

Make sure you send your letter
RSVP.

Conjuring Pleasure

MAKE A VOW to bring forth all your sensual power. You will radiate passion and be intensely drawn to your lover. Perform this ritual at the next full moon.

Collect:

◇ **essential oils**

◇ **candles**

◇ **drink of your choice**

Begin with a blissful bath in oil-scented water. Sit in a darkened room. Raise a cup of jasmine tea, a glass of wine, or whatever your special drink is and speak this spell aloud:

Now I awaken the Goddess in me.
I surrender to love's power.
Tonight I will heat the night
with my fire.
As I drink this cup,
my juices flower.
I am alive! I am love! And so it is.

Tantric Tryst

T O STRENGTHEN the closeness between you and a lover, plan a special evening on the next full moon. Blend together the following resins:

◇ One part amber
◇ One part sandalwood
◇ One part frankincense

This Eastern Wisdom mix may well have been used by Cleopatra when she and Marc Antony made mad love on the banks of the Nile. Add four generous drops of gardenia and grind the mixture together. In a bowl, light the ground mixture.

Remove your lover's clothes and walk around him holding the smoking incense bowl to bless his physical body. Then, he should remove your clothes and circle you, in your full glory, with the incense.

Now, speak the following "full moon blessing" together. Or you can do it before your lover arrives, if you prefer, but the spell is more powerful with both of your intentions intertwined.

With every word,
I draw you closer to me.
With every breath,
I do you embrace.
Tonight we bind our hearts.
Tonight we twine our bodies.
So mote it be.

Place the incense beside your bed and sit facing each other, eyes open. With the lightest possible touch, brush your finger on

his skin, starting with the face
and working your way down.
Go very slowly. It should take at
least a half hour for this "tantric
touch." Then you should please
each other manually while still
looking in each other's eyes. At
this point, anything can happen—
and should!

Spellbinding Seduction:

CORDS OF CONNECTION

FOR HEIGHTENED and sustained sensual pleasure, try this sacred spell. Take two goblets, two "Fire and Ice" red and white roses, and a yard of red thread. Sprinkle a dash of nutmeg in each goblet. Uncork a bottle of fine red wine for later, allowing it to breathe.

With red ink and a slip of paper, write your lover's name on the paper and what your hopes and intentions are for the night. Let your imagination run wild here. Take the red thread and recite this as you tie each knot:

With a knot of one,
this spell is begun.
Knot number two,
for me and for you.
Knot number three,
you come to me.
Knot number four,
your knock upon my door.
Knot number five,
our passion comes alive.

Anoint the red thread with one drop of the red wine and one drop of rose oil. Tie the red thread around your waist and place the parchment under your bed.

Welcome your lover at the door with a glass of wine and a bowl of strawberries, wearing only the red thread.

Wear the magic cord until it falls off, usually after 30 days.

Kama Sutra Kiss

THE KISS is the gateway to bliss and amorous experiences. The kiss provokes sensual ardor, excites the heart, and is an incitation to the natural gift of yourself that you share with your beloved. Here is a list of actual Kama Sutra kisses:

Bent kiss: the classic movie kiss where lovers lean into each other in this classic kiss

Throbbing kiss: the woman touches her lover's lips with her tongue and eyes and places her hands on her lover's hands

Turned kiss: one kisser turns up the face of the other by holding the head and chin and then kissing

Pressed kiss: the one lover from below or underneath presses the lower lip from above with both lips

Greatly pressed kiss: taking the lip between two fingers, touching the lip with the tongue, and then applying great pressure with the lips upon lips in the kiss

Yohimbe Root Tea Ritual

CENTURIES BEFORE there was Viagra, there was yohimbe root, now commonly sold in health food stores. Yohimbe is a very potent, natural way to maximize your love interest's vigor before a special night.

First make incense by blending together:

◇ One part sandalwood
◇ One part myrrh
◇ One part yohimbe root
◇ Three drops tuberose oil

Light the incense and burn it while brewing your yohimbe root tea.

Speak the following aloud:

Lover of my heart,
my passion I impart.
Love of my flesh,
my passion is fresh.
Lover of my mind,
your passion to me binds.

Breakup Ritual

T O RID YOURSELF of negative emotions after a fight or the end of a relationship, try this purification bath. Draw a warm bath at noon when the sun is at its healing peak, and add these essential oils into the water as it flows from the faucet:

◇ two drops rosemary *(for calm)*
◇ one drop peppermint *(for stimulation)*
◇ one drop lavender *(for energy cleansing)*
◇ three drops thyme *(to relieve mental exhaustion)*

As you soak and steam, repeat this prayer four times:

Sadness, I release you—goodbye.
Fatigue, I release you—goodbye.
I greet this day anew,
I greet my life renewed.
Blessed be.

Romantic Woes:
BURN AWAY
BAD LUCK IN LOVE

PERHAPS YOU HAVE been over-whelmed recently by a series of unfortunate events in love and romance, seemingly beyond your control. Do away with these burdens as quickly as possible. This spell requires: paper, a black candle, a flat rock with a hollow in the center to set the candle into, peppermint oil, peony blossom, a black ink pen, and a "cancellation" stamp, readily available at any stationery store.

Anoint your candle with a drop of peppermint oil. Dress your altar with a peony blossom, the luckiest of the flower family. The consummate time to release bad luck is immediately after the full moon. Write on a piece of parchment or stationery what you wish to be freed from; this is your "release request." Write this same request onto the candle, as well. Ideally, this is scratched into the candle with the thorn of a rose you have grown yourself. Light the candle near an open window so the negative energy will leave your home. While the candle burns, intone:

Waxing moon,
most wise Cybele,
From me this burden
please dispel.
Upon this night so clear
and bright
I release ____ to the
moon tonight.

Burn the candle for thirteen
minutes. Take your stamp and
mark the paper "cancelled." Put

the candle out, fold the paper away from you, and place it under the candle stone. Repeat this process for thirteen nights. On the last night, which should be the beginning of the New Moon phase, burn the paper and bury the candle, paper ashes, and rock far from your home. Give thanks to the moon for assisting you, and let go of bad luck.

The Power
of Love

AS A HEALER, you will some-
times perform spells for
those who are not present.
You can set up another altar to
represent the recipient of your
magic or have candles dedicated
to the ailing one.

Begin by setting up two altar candles—one in the northeast and one in the northwest. Light them, then place three red candles on the east side of your altar and one orange candle on the west. The red candles stand for health and strength, while the orange candle lights the way for optimism and encouragement.

Light the orange candle and concentrate on attracting good health, love, and good feeling.

Next, light all three red candles
and think of vitality and increasing
the flow of energy while you recite:

Power of Light, Power of Love,
The fire burns and we heal.

Peace, Love, and Healing

THE ULTIMATE ALCHEMY is to generate positive energy that spirals outward, improving everything in its path. I know of shamans and wise women who have dedicated their lives to doing good works, including some crones who practice in the ancient rainforest to protect the trees, and aborigines who spend their "dreamtime" repairing the Earth. You can contribute to universal peace and healing by burning a white candle, anointed with rose oil, on your altar during a waning moon on Saturday, Saturn's Day.

Place a single white rose in water and lay a garlic clove

beside some rose incense. Light
the incense, then take a bundle
of white sage, light the end, and
pass the smoke over your altar to
"smudge" the space. Chant:

War and grief will come
to an end,
We walk the path of peace.
Love thy neighbor as thyself,
All we need is love.
With harm to none, only
understanding.

This book has been bound using handcraft methods and Smyth-sewn to ensure durability.

Designed by Susan Van Horn.

Edited by Jennifer Leczkowski.

The text was set in Lomba, Black Knight, and Abraham Lincoln.

Images provided by Thinkstock.
ART CREDITS— p.15: milalala; p.21,25,89: art12321; p.29: Photos.com; p.44: Annasivak, p.57: RiSem; p.60: Crowoman; p.94: la_puma; p.104, p.118: ArtnerDluxe; p.106: asmakar; p.111: Concluserat; p.114: Ela Kwasniewski; p.138: mart_m; p.158, p.164: kameshkova; header decorative elements: Yevgeniy Il\'yin